ONE-LINERS FROM GOD

Biblical Affirmations
To Lift Up The Heart

The Fun Nun®
Sister Mary Christelle Macaluso, RSM, OFN, PhD

web site: www.funnun.com
FUN NUN® BOOKS
COLLEGE OF SAINT MARY
OMAHA, NEBRASKA USA 68124-2377

Scripture quotations are taken from The Living Bible copyright © 1971. Used by permission of Tyndale House Publishers, Inc., Wheaton, Illinois 60189. All Rights Reserved.

Layout by Shirley Trout
Cover Design by Carol Sayers
Printed in the United States of America by Moran Printing, Omaha, Nebraska

15 14 13 12 11 10 9 8 7 6 5 4 3 2 1

Copyright© 1999 by The Fun Nun®, Sister M. Christelle Macaluso, RSM, OFN, PhD
Library of Congress Catalog Card Number: 99-90612
ISBN: 0-9663462-1-1

Publisher: Fun Nun® Books
             College of Saint Mary
             Omaha, Nebraska USA 68124-2377
             Phone: 402-399-2474 FAX: 402-399-2686
             Email: funnun@csm.edu
             Web Site: www.funnun.com

DEDICATION

To all those who are seeking to grow spiritually.

To all those who are looking for a deeper meaning in life.

To all those who are looking for God.

To all those who have found God.

ACKNOWLEDGMENTS

No book ever comes to completion without the involvement of many people. Surely this book is no exception. I am grateful to Carol Corey. From the very first day she shared my vision, encouraged me, and worked endlessly along the way. I'm indebted to Shirley Trout, author of *Light Dances* (1997), who shared her gifts with me in so many ways — especially her insights and her professional knowledge about writing books. I also want to thank her for the lovely layout of the book. I also have my friend, Roberta Milford, to thank for the title of this book, and the Sisters of Mercy who have always encouraged my endeavors. I am grateful to Carol Sayers for her design of the cover of this book. I appreciate the College of Saint Mary for all its support, and Polly Nimmer, Sister Dolores Preisinger, RSM, and Carol Corey for their editorial advice. Thanks to my family and friends who supported my goals and to any of you I may have forgotten.

ABOUT THE AUTHOR

Sister Mary Christelle Macaluso, RSM, OFN, PhD, better known as "The Fun Nun®," has been a full time professional speaker since 1980. She teaches people how to live more joyfully and reduce their stress levels. She speaks nationally and internationally to business, health, education, government, religious, and social groups. The Fun Nun® has been on many radio talk shows and has appeared on national television. She is a member of the National Speakers Association.

Before becoming a professional speaker, The Fun Nun® taught for 16 years at College of Saint Mary in Omaha, Nebraska. Her educational background includes a BS from College of Saint Mary, an MS from the University of Notre Dame, and a PhD from the University of Nebraska.

The Fun Nun is planning on several books from these two series, *One-Liners From God* and *God Knows Best About....* If you want more details about her forthcoming books, please contact her.

The Order of the Fun Nuns (OFN), founded by her, has thousands of members. Members are encouraged to spread some joy each day in their own way. There is a membership card for you on the next page.

The Fun Nun® will make you laugh while you are learning! She speaks on topics related to humor, stress, and self-image. If you need to add some life and zest to your program, invite The Fun Nun®! Contact her by any of the following ways:

Phone:	402-399-2474 Fax: 402-399-2686
Email:	funnun@csm.edu
Web Site:	www.funnun.com
Address:	College of Saint Mary
	1901 S. 72nd St.
	Omaha, NE USA 68124-2377

MEMBERSHIP CARD

ORDER OF THE FUN NUNS (OFN)
OPEN TO ALL

A MERRY HEART DOES LIKE GOOD MEDICINE
PROVERBS 17:22

I, _____,
SPREAD SOME JOY EACH DAY IN MY OWN WAY.

THE FUN NUN®
SISTER M. CHRISTELLE MACALUSO, RSM, OFN, PhD
COLLEGE OF SAINT MARY, 1901 S. 72ND ST., OMAHA, NE 68124-2377
402-399-2474, FAX: 402-399-2686, EMAIL: funnun@csm.edu
WEB SITE: www.funnun.com

Introduction

The Bible is a wealth of wisdom. Its words need to be in your heart to nourish your soul. My book, *One-Liners From God*, contains Biblical passages and affirmations derived from these verses. Reflecting on the verses and repeating the affirmations will strengthen your faith.

There are many passages in the Bible which lend themselves to affirmations. This is the first book of an intended series that will share verses and affirmations with you.

I chose *The Living Bible* because the translation uses words and expressions that agree with common parlance.

My prayer is that you may grow in the love of God as you ponder the words in this book.

The Fun Nun®
Sister Mary Christelle Macaluso, RSM, OFN, PhD
College of Saint Mary, Omaha, Nebraska USA

ONE-LINERS FROM GOD

THE FUN NUN®

SISTER MARY CHRISTELLE MACALUSO, RSM, OFN, PhD

God protected them
in the howling wilderness
as though they were
the apple of his eye.

Deuteronomy 32:10

One-Liners From God

I am the apple of God's eye.

*You made all the delicate,
inner parts of my body,
and knit them together
in my mother's womb.
Thank you for making me
so wonderfully complex!...*

Psalm 139:13-14

One-Liners From God

I am a wonderful person!

6

"Sir, which is the most important command in the laws of Moses?"
Jesus replied,
"Love the Lord your God with all your heart, soul, and mind. This is the first and greatest commandment."

Matthew 22:36-38

I love God with my whole heart, soul, and mind.

**"The second most important
is similar:
'Love your neighbor
as much as you love yourself.' "**

Matthew 22:39

I love my neighbor as myself.

9

*You shall give
due honor and respect
to the elderly
in the fear of God.
I am Jehovah.*

Leviticus 19:32

I respect the elderly.

Take care to live in me,
and let me live in you.
For a branch can't produce fruit
when severed from the vine.
Nor can you be fruitful
apart from me.

John 15:4

I live in Christ and He lives in me.

> ..."Oh, have mercy on us
> and do something if you can."
> "If I can?" Jesus asked.
> "Anything is possible
> if you have faith."

Mark 9:22-23

I have a deep faith.

*Let there be tears
for the wrong things
you have done.
Let there be sorrow
and sincere grief...*

James 4:9

One-Liners From God

I am sorry for all the wrong I have done.

*For God has bought you
with a great price.
So use every part of your body
to give glory back to God,
because he owns it.*

1 Corinthians 6:20

One-Liners From God

My whole being gives glory back to God.

**But you, dear friends,
must build up your lives
ever more strongly
upon the foundation of our holy faith,
learning to pray
in the power and strength
of the Holy Spirit.**

Jude 1:20

I build my life centered on faith.

21

**He personally carried the load
of our sins in his own body
when he died on the cross,
so that we can be finished with sin
and live a good life from now on.
For his wounds have healed ours!**

1 Peter 2:24

I am healed by Christ's wounds.

If you want to know what God wants you to do,
ask him, and he will gladly tell you,
for he is always ready
to give a bountiful supply of wisdom
to all who ask him; he will not resent it...
If you don't ask with faith,
don't expect the Lord
to give you any solid answer.

James 1:5,8

I ask God to know His will.

> *Most of all, let love guide your life,*
> *for then the whole church*
> *will stay together*
> *in perfect harmony.*

Colossians 3:14

I let love be my guide.

I will instruct you
(says the Lord)
and guide you
along the best pathway
for your life;
I will advise you
and watch your progress.

Psalm 32:8

One-Liners From God

God is always watching over me.

*A good man's mind
is filled with honest thoughts;
an evil man's mind
is crammed with lies.*

Proverbs 12:5

I fill my mind with honest thoughts.

But your heavenly Father
already knows perfectly well
that you need them
(food and clothing),
and he will give them to you
if you give him first place in your life
and live as he wants you to.

Matthew 6:32-33

I give God first place in my life.

"Go back to your family,"
he told him,
"and tell them
what a wonderful thing
God has done for you."

Luke 8:39

I thank God for the blessings He has given me.

*But it is no shame to suffer
for being a Christian.
Praise God for the privilege
of being in Christ's family
and being called
by his wonderful name!*

1 Peter 4:16

One-Liners From God

I am proud to be called a Christian.

*Now you are no longer strangers
to God and foreigners to heaven,
but you are members
of God's very own family,
citizens of God's country,
and you belong in God's household
with every other Christian.*

Ephesians 2:19

One-Liners From God

I am a member of God's family.

For God is at work within you,
helping you want to obey him,
and then
helping you do what he wants.

Philippians 2:13

God is at work within me.

How constantly I find myself
upon the verge of sin,
this source of sorrow
always stares me in the face.
I confess my sins;
I am sorry for what I have done.

Psalm 38:17-18

One-Liners From God

I confess my sins, and am sorry for them.

43

*God delights in those
who keep their promises,
and abhors those who don't.*

Proverbs 12:22

I keep the promises I make.

*Ask, and you will be given
what you ask for.
Seek, and you will find.
Knock, and the door will be opened.*

Matthew 7:7

I ask
that I may receive.

47

Feed the flock of God;
care for it willingly, not grudgingly;
not for what you will get out of it,
but because you are eager
to serve the Lord.

1 Peter 5:2

I am eager to serve the Lord.

■ ■ ■ ■ ■ ■ ■ ■ ■ ■ ■ ■ ■ ■ ■ ■

*And God has reserved for his children
the priceless gift of eternal life;
it is kept in heaven for you,
pure and undefiled,
beyond the reach of change and decay...
So be truly glad!
There is wonderful joy ahead,
even though the going is rough
for a while down here.*

1 Peter 1:4,6

One-Liners From God

My real home is in heaven.

51

**God's purpose in this
was that we should praise God
and give glory to him
for doing these mighty things for us,
who were the first to trust in Christ.**

Ephesians 1:12

I praise God and give Him glory.

54

Heal the sick,
raise the dead,
cure the lepers,
and cast out demons.
Give as freely as you have received!

Matthew 10:8

I am a generous person.

O Lord my God,
many and many a time you have done
great miracles for us,
and we are ever in your thoughts.
Who else can do such glorious things?
There isn't time
to tell of all your wonderful deeds.

Psalm 40:5

One-Liners From God

I am always in God's thoughts.

*So I saw that there is
nothing better for men
than that they should be
happy in their work,
for that is what they are here for,
and no one can bring them back to life
to enjoy what will be in the future,
so let them enjoy it now.*

Ecclesiastes 3:22

One-Liners From God

I am happy in my work.

**Anxious hearts
are very heavy
but a word of encouragement
does wonders!**

Proverbs 12:25

I give words of encouragement.

61

These trials
are only to test your faith,
to see whether or not
it is strong and pure.
It is being tested
as fire tests gold and purifies it,
and your faith is
far more precious to God
than mere gold...

1 Peter 1:7

One-Liners From God

My faith remains strong in difficult times.

..."Then who in the world
can be saved?" they asked.
Jesus looked at them intently
and said,
"Humanly speaking, no one.
But with God,
everything is possible."

Matthew 19:25-26

One-Liners From God

I know that, with God, all things are possible.

65

And I pray that Christ
will be more and more at home
in your hearts,
living within you as you trust in him.
May your roots
go down deep into the soil
of God's marvelous love.

Ephesians 3:17

One-Liners From God

My roots grow deep into the soil of God's love.

*...Fix your thoughts
on what is true and good and right.
Think about things
that are pure and lovely,
and dwell on the fine,
good things in others.
Think about all you can praise God for
and be glad about.*

Philippians 4:8

One-Liners From God

I watch over my thoughts and think positively.

**But as for me,
I get as close to him as I can!
I have chosen him
and I will tell everyone
about the wonderful ways
he rescues me.**

Psalm 73:28

I am close to God.

Happy are those whose hearts are pure, for they shall see God.

Matthew 5:8

I
am
pure.

Pride leads to arguments;
be humble,
take advice
and become wise.

Proverbs 13:10

I listen wisely to advice.

75

Be humble and gentle.
Be patient with each other,
making allowance
for each other's faults
because of your love.

Ephesians 4:2

I make allowances for others' faults.

For as you know him better,
he will give you,
through his great power,
everything you need
for living a truly good life:
he even shares his own glory
and his own goodness with us!

2 Peter 1:3

I have everything I need
to live a good life.

It is good to say, "Thank you"
to the Lord,
to sing praises to the God
who is above all gods.
Every morning tell him,
"Thank you for your kindness,"
and every evening
rejoice in all his faithfulness.

Psalm 92:1-2

One-Liners From God

I thank the Lord each day.

So if you are standing
before the altar in the Temple,
offering a sacrifice to God,
and suddenly remember
that a friend has something against you,
leave your sacrifice there beside the altar
and go and apologize and be reconciled to him,
and then come and offer your sacrifice to God.

Matthew 5:23-24

One-Liners From God

I apologize for any wrong I have done.

Everyone enjoys giving good advice,
and how wonderful it is
to be able to say
the right thing
at the right time!

Proverbs 15:23

I say the right thing at the right time.

Seek the Lord
while you can find him.
Call upon him now while he is near.

Isaiah 55:6

I seek the Lord always.

If you want a happy, good life,
keep control of your tongue,
and guard your lips
from telling lies.
Turn away from evil and do good...

1 Peter 3:10-11

I guard my lips from telling lies.

90

Don't store up treasures here on earth
where they can erode away
and may be stolen.
Store them in heaven
where they will never lose their value,
and are safe from thieves.
If your profits are in heaven
your heart will be there too.

Matthew 6: 19-21

One-Liners From God

I store up treasures in heaven.

...Rejoice before the Lord your God in everything you do.

Deuteronomy 12:18

I rejoice in my God.

Dear friends,
while you are waiting for these
things to happen for him to come,
try hard to live without sinning;
and be at peace with everyone
so that he will be pleased with you
when he returns.

2 Peter 3:14

I live in peace with everyone.

95

Don't criticize,
and then you won't be criticized.
For others will treat you
as you treat them.

Matthew 7:1-2

I say positive things about others.

Now your attitudes and thoughts
must all be constantly changing
for the better.
Yes, you must be
a new and different person,
holy and good.
Clothe yourself with this new nature.

Ephesians 4:23-24

One-Liners From God

My attitudes and thoughts change constantly for the better.

*You will be judged
on whether or not you are doing
what Christ wants you to.
So watch what you do
and what you think.*

James 2:12

I watch over my thoughts and actions.

Love forgets mistakes;
nagging about them
parts the best of friends.

Proverbs 17:9

One-Liners From God

I forget others' mistakes and my own.

If anyone is stealing
he must stop it
and begin using those hands of his
for honest work
so he can give to others in need.

Ephesians 4:28

I use my hands for honest work.

*So many say
that God will never help me.
But Lord, you are my shield,
my glory, and my only hope.
You alone can lift my head,
now bowed in shame.*

Psalm 3:2-3

I place my hope in God.

*...And don't you realize
that you also will perish
unless you leave evil ways
and turn to God?*

Luke 13:3

I give up my sinful ways and turn to God.

Little children, let us stop
just saying we love people;
let us really love them,
and show it by our actions.

1 John 3:18

I show
I love others
by my actions.

111

**Be careful —
watch out for attacks from Satan,
your great enemy.
He prowls around
like a hungry, roaring lion,
looking for some victim to tear apart.
Stand firm when he attacks...**

1 Peter 5:8-9

I stand firm in the Lord when Satan tempts me.

*A true friend is always loyal,
and a brother is born to help
in time of need.*

Proverbs 17:17

One-Liners From God

I am a loyal and true friend.

Don't use bad language.
Say only what is good and helpful
to those you are talking to,
and what will give them a blessing.

Ephesians 4:29

I say only what is good and helpful.

117

*But Jesus ignored their comments
and said to Jairus,
"Don't be afraid.
Just trust me."*

Mark 5:36

I am not afraid because I trust in God.

Stand before the Lord in awe,
and do not sin against him.
Lie quietly upon your bed
in silent meditation.
Put your trust in the Lord...

Psalm 4:4-5

I stand in awe before the Lord.

**Anyone who says he is a Christian
but doesn't control
his sharp tongue
is just fooling himself,
and his religion isn't worth much.**

James 1:26

I control my tongue.

123

...And as for others,
help them to find the Lord
by being kind to them,
but be careful that you yourselves
aren't pulled along into their sins.
Hate every trace of their sin
while being merciful to them as sinners.

Jude 1:23

I am kind and merciful.

125

Always be full of joy in the Lord; I say it again, rejoice!

Philippians 4:4

I am full of joy in the Lord.

And I, the King, will tell them,
"When you did it to these
my brothers,
you were doing it to me!"

Matthew 25:40

I see Christ in others and treat them with love and respect.

**Dear brothers,
don't ever forget
that it is best to listen much,
speak little, and not become angry;
for anger doesn't make us good,
as God demands that we must be.**

James 1:19

I am a good person.

131

> *...O Lord my God,*
> *I will keep thanking you*
> *forever!*

Psalm 30:12

One-Liners From God

I give thanks to God.

133

> ***...be kind to each other, tenderhearted, forgiving one another, just as God has forgiven you because you belong to Christ.***
>
> Ephesians 4:32

I forgive others as God has forgiven me.

You are my hiding place
from every storm of life;
you even keep me
from getting into trouble!

Psalm 32:7

God is my strength in all my problems.

But the wisdom that comes from heaven
is first of all pure
and full of quiet gentleness.
Then it is peace-loving and courteous.
It allows discussion
and is willing to yield to others,
it is full of mercy and good deeds...

James 3:17

One-Liners From God

I am peace-loving and courteous.

**For though once
your heart was full of darkness,
now it is full of light from the Lord,
and your behavior should show it!
Because of this light within you,
you should do only what is
good and right and true.**

Ephesians 5:8-9

One-Liners From God

I act justly and do what is right.

***The Kingdom of God
is not just talking;
it is living by God's power.***

1 Corinthians 4:20

I live
by God's power.

143

*I will praise the Lord
no matter what happens.
I will constantly speak
of his glories and grace.
I will boast of all his kindness to me.
Let all who are discouraged take heart.
Let us praise the Lord together,
and exalt his name.*

Psalm 34:1-3

One-Liners From God

I praise the Lord each day.

145

146

For unless you are honest in small matters,
you won't be in large ones.
If you cheat even a little,
you won't be honest
with greater responsibilities.
And if you are untrustworthy
about worldly wealth,
who will trust you
with the true riches of heaven?

Luke 16:10-11

One-Liners From God

I am honest in large and small matters.

147

*Admit your faults to one another
and pray for each other
so that you may be healed.
The earnest prayer of a righteous man
has great power and wonderful results.*

James 5:16

One-Liners From God

I pray for others.

*Commit everything you do
to the Lord.
Trust him to help you do it
and he will.*

Psalm 37:5

One-Liners From God

I commit everything I do to the Lord.

*I call heaven and earth
to witness against you
that today I have set before you
life or death,
blessing or curse.
Oh, that you would choose life,
that you and your children might live!*

Deuteronomy 30:19

I choose life!

**For in Christ
here is all of God in a human body,
so you have everything
when you have Christ,
and you are filled with God
through your union with Christ.
He is the highest Ruler,
with authority over every other power.**

Colossians 2:9-10

One-Liners From God

I have everything when I have Christ.

155

I will sing to the Lord
as long as I live.
I will praise God to my last breath!
May he be pleased
by all these thoughts about him,
for he is the source of my joy.

Psalm 104:33-34

One-Liners From God

I will praise God to my last breath!

Long ago, even before he made the world,
God chose us to be his very own,
through what Christ would do for us;
he decided then
to make us holy in his eyes,
without a single fault —
we who stand before him
covered with his love.

Ephesians 1:4

One-Liners From God

I stand before God, covered with His love.

159

*My plea is not for the world
but for those you have given me
because they belong to you.
And all of them, since they are mine,
belong to you;
and you have given them back to me
with everything else of yours,
and so they are my glory!*

John 17:9-10

One-Liners From God

I am the glory of Christ!

**See how very much
our heavenly Father loves us,
for he allows us to be called
his children —
think of it — and we really are!...**

1 John 3:1

I am a child of God! Alleluia! Alleluia!

BIBLE VERSES USED
OLD TESTAMENT

Deuteronomy	12:18, 30:19, 32:10
Ecclesiastes	3:22
Isaiah	55:6
Leviticus	19:32
Proverbs	12:5, 12:22, 12:25, 13:10, 15:23, 17:9, 17:17
Psalms	3:2-3, 4:4-5, 30:12, 32:7, 32:8, 34:1-3, 37:5, 38:17-18, 40:5, 73:28, 92:1-2, 104:33-34, 139:13-14

One-Liners From God

BIBLE VERSES USED
NEW TESTAMENT

Colossians	2:9-10, 3:14
1 Corinthians	4:20, 6:20
Ephesians	1:4, 1:12, 2:19, 3:17, 4:2, 4:23-24, 4:28, 4:29, 4:32, 5:8-9
James	1:5,8, 1:19, 1:26, 2:12, 3:17, 4:9, 5:16
John	15:4, 17:9-10
1 John	3:1, 3:18
Jude	1:20, 1:23
Luke	8:39, 13:3, 16:10-11
Mark	5:36, 9:22-23
Matthew	5:8, 5:23-24, 6:19-21, 6:32-33, 7:1-2, 7:7, 10:8, 19:25-26, 22:36-38, 22:39, 25:40
1 Peter	1:4,6, 1:7, 2:24, 3:10-11, 4:16, 5:2, 5:8-9
2 Peter	1:3, 3:14
Philippians	2:13, 4:4, 4:8

One-Liners From God

One-Liners From God

BOOK ORDER FORM

One-liners from God	$9.95
God Knows Best About Joy	$9.95
Postage and Handling per book	$2.00

Send check or money order (**in USA currency**) made payable to *Sisters of Mercy*. Mail with form to: Fun Nun Books, College of Saint Mary, 1901 S. 72nd St., Omaha, NE USA 68124-2377.

Your Name: _____

Company: _____

Address: _____

City: _____ State: _____

Country: _____ Zip: _____

Telephone: _____ Fax: _____

Email: _____

$11.95 X _____ Book(s) = Total: _____

THANK YOU FOR YOUR ORDER!

One-Liners From God

FUN NUN CASSETTE TAPE ORDER FORM

Cost per tape, including postage $11.00

_____ Laughter/Jokes/Laughter

_____ Wellness and Your Funny Bone

_____ The Merry Christian

_____ Self-image and Interpersonal Relationships

_____ Communication and Interpersonal Relationships

_____ Stress: What's It All About?

_____ Relaxation Techniques

_____ The Mind/Body Connection

$11.00 X_____ = Total_____

Send check or money order (in U.S. currency) made payable to: **Sisters of Mercy**.
Mail form with the information on page 170 to:
The Fun Nun, College of Saint Mary, 1901 S. 72 St., Omaha, NE USA, 68124-2377
THANK YOU FOR YOUR ORDER!

Please send the tapes indicated on page 169 to:

Your Name: _____

Company: _____

Address: _____

City: _____ State: _____

Country: _____ Zip: _____

Telephone: _____ Fax: _____

Email: _____